Awash with Violets

A book of verse with home on the horizon
by

Roisin Veronica Horgan

Publishing partner: Paragon Publishing, Rothersthorpe

ISBN 978-1-78222-912-4

Book design, layout and production management by Into Print
www.intoprint.net

+44 (0)1604 832149

Dedicated to my mother Frances

CONTENTS

No Man's Land

Offshore Islands like tug boats on the Shannon
pull me into the mythical world of '*Diarmuid agus Grainne*'.
Peering down from Moher
the sea batters this lonesome rock
like time dismantling memory.
A robin red breast beats beneath a harp shaped cloud.
Bidding me to listen to more than wind.
To look inwards not backwards
to bare souls baring their scars
and not the flag flying.

I step down from a limestone bed
stretched out by a driving ice sheet
as sharp as emerald.
Onto the green of St. Brigid's cloak
unfolded for my protection and my kin.
I am directed by the master at the hedge
across cutaway bog
that would smoulder still
under a blackened pot.
If a battering ram
hadn't thrown native fledglings from their nest.
To perish in the fields
like the potato furrows
wherein their hope had died.

Saints now.

Looking down on
emigrants returned as presidents.
Spying their reflection on the Áras silver.
(Áras meaning the President of Ireland's house)
And I curl a wet Big Issue into my bag.
I relate
but hide in the unspeak
with my ancestors.
Who bid me to
close handsome annals
laying testimony to how they danced at the crossroads
and amber fires like banner flags flew.
And the Dalcais roamed looking out over Killaloe
for fawn and foe
like Davy and the lads.
And feel the tempo
of living souls
who cannot find their verse.

The lighthouse shone on the Loop
for those who came and went
but it was the round towers
like the one on Scattery
that shone a light within.
When we were driven
where that little Arc stood.
Where all the lost make their home
when they have nothing,
only their '*paidreacha*' (prayers)
on no man's land.

Being Young in Ballybeg

Shaped like a toblerone boat
tweaked by my mother's hand
awash with violets
centred in a moat of memory
next to Ballybeg wood.
I loved it from the inside.
Gazing into the amber flames and fearing hell
the hearth rose like a battleship
little I knew of war.
A bounty of Waterford cut glass
yodelling crystal and a shape of lamp light shadow.
Every dream
my mother and I shared
that never perished to ash
leans against that stone edifice
still.
Cocooned.
The eldest child
on a softly greying mohair rug.
Listening to a low cough.
Fluff sticking to corduroy.
The static never quite finished with me.
Beside a red rimmed table
dapper like my father.
I could barely see through the fog.
Its underlay
a painted map of Éire.

I didn't know there were
two parts tethered
with rushing strokes.

I was a home bird
and Ballybeg had built a nest in my heart.
When the oak table was lifted in front of the fire at Christmas.
I wished it would stay
festive and detached.
My heart shattered on shiny new delph
as the reality of
the paramilitaries and their bombs
was beamed into my developing conscience.
Tough blokes who wouldn't heed the Pope's peace.
Widows and little ones losing their edifice
in a white washed mortuary.
Like the one at the back of the county hospital
where cars still rushed past
with unbowed heads in the driver's seat
shopping on a Sunday.
There were names but faces we were never supposed to see.
I wondered who was part of a faction.
I didn't know if I was good.
The furniture was put back on the 6th and the curtains opened.
The light seemed strange.
It faltered on the littlest cloud.
Not like the steady light and shadow that I was accustomed to.
Its reverberation missed still.
Summer came and we moved away.

Yet I still see the world awash with violets
through that tall window.
Divided into teak manageable squares
like the chapters of my living.
I watch the drops.
Redirecting them as if I am steering that same toblerone boat
with youthful exuberance.
It is all the home I need
when there is nothing sweet
only a dusting of memory and being good.

The Hills are Decloaked

The hills are decloaked of their troubles.
Yesterday is washed into the sea at Clogher Road.
Words rush to embrace me
like safe stepping stones.
I climb to stand on common ground
on the mountain of Callan.
Sure footed in the steps of my ancestors.
Following emotional rivers to the source.
Intertwined hands provide balance.
Journey's end is not on the horizon.
The view spans out over limestone plains
as far as the heart can see.
On a mountain of many, many surprises.

Cowslips

After a downpour
the dunnock bird hops.
Puddles collapse mud dams.
Deep imprints of inherited boots
lift forward.
Cowslips almost trampled
dressed in deep majestic yellow
crest on the flow.
A fleeting bow of colour that a cow could dash.
Like a baby tooth
pushed up through the gums of the earth.
A garnish
at your buckled heel that could lay bare the heart of any table.

Strawberry Jam

Strawberry jam was always low
at night
after the prayers.
Brown bread cut into thick squares
too fresh to toast.
The golden sun setting behind the still
waters of the marina.
The purple stained glass in the hall
feeling none of its warmth.
This three storey house stooped
neck tie tight.
Filling me with flexes of artificial light.
Moonlight behind a white lace veil
sort of set my sail
And so I crossed the road
for jam.

It was the wind that swept me.
Fates indeterminable push.
A rush.
To rush back home.
Or perchance to try to see deeper.
Out past the crumbling cliffs of memory.
Out past the worry trees uprooted and about to attack
pulling me back.
The bell jingles and I giggle
a little triumph to be free
walking in as teenage me.

A muddied bus puffs and screeches from the square.
The town hall, a theatre to a foreigner's dream, stands austere.
And I below the bows of a hazel tree
none the wise.

I go home by bus in June.
High tide.
The boats are tethered low.
Pulled by an acute tug.
There is a thrombosis of sorts.
On the street between two worlds.
With a walking stick in hand.
Sailing almost free.
I hold my chest then wave my arms
like paddles into the deep

crossing the road for jam.

Incommunicado

The sweetness of language
like whipped cream
melting into a dry tongue.
A cacophony of thoughts,
like buds to reason in an instant.
The lost feelings quavering,
the sudden staccato of excitement arresting
and the eyes in a playful duet
like fledglings somersaulting
in an upward current.
Innocence
detaching from the mind
and travelling,
to an awakening ear,
as if to translate a bird song.
Serenading, swooping
and eclipsed by a bitter reply
as if my words were an arrow
shot from a warped bow.

Returning in the Memory

In hazy sunshine
the mist dances into the west
awakening the past.
Like a breeze through a sash squeezed open.
White garlic flowers alight my senses
freeing memories of my aunt's house.
Foul incessantly pecking and waddling.
Their extended necks almost up to my armpits
ready to devour me.
A smother of native hazel circling the yard.
It clacked like raw wool on a loom.
The wind was from the North.
I wanted to stay inside and search the dresser.
For clues of when she was me.
Young.

For ancient crosses and holy water.
Lilac hair rollers and secret tins.
Soft velvet boxes that still spring with delight.
A mirror aged with silver rivets catching a glint of a beauty
A satin headscarf in a diamond fold.
Soft stitching on embroidery of the greenest hills.
Sore creative fingers dancing on a whistle.
And I chasing ivory ribbon and backing onto subsiding flags.
Encrusted with rough red embers.

Warmth for frosty nights
when heavy pots needed to boil
and fires never quenched.

Like old joints creaking suddenly.
I could fall into her mother's time.
Feeling the normality of someone else's sanctuary.
Inedible purple heather and lush green give way
to a wet tea cloth unfurling cut after cut of soda bread
that moors me by the fire.
As hurled turf splinters on the grate.
The sun like an oil lamp is turned down
letting loose the shadows.

A rocking chair denotes the speed of silence
the speed of memory.
The night deepens each blink until my eyelids surrender
and I am tipped into the car.
A blast of heat from the car battery and suddenly
We are reversing, spinning and re-entering the world again.
Leaving loose buttercups on her dresser and a forgotten parcel of
duck eggs and a hedge full of sloes picked to perfection.
Decades later I can still imagine her and I, as two young girls.
My knuckles banging on her thin glass door louder than the
hoarse drake.
Her glasses swinging on an inherited chain
and our minds laden with promises like her dresser.

The Moon Bends

I know where the lamps are in the sky.
And how the moon bends
behind the old chimney.
Like the north star
hovering above the drain
that flows by the sunken ditch.
The bramble like tangled Christmas lights missing a fuse
glistens in a translucent over-coat of dew.
Something moves a twig.
I glided clear over it
when I was only inches out of the mud.
And now it coddles the field like an old bobbled cardigan.
Laden with waxy berries for the speckled finches
if we see the dawn.

I know where the sun sets in the low of January.
Like youths shy beam
shimmering but not for long.

Courage is Driftwood

Courage is driftwood on a wave.
Ship wrecked caravan of the sea.
Stripped of excess
held high on the crest.
The rocks, the rocks.
Fearless now.
Beached bliss.

Fairy Cakes

Fairy cakes steam straight from the oven.
Soft sponge bounces back against the gentle caress
of floured hands
dusted with icing sugar for messy children.
Green grass waves at me
from my easy chair at the kitchen table.
I escape to the garden unnoticed.
Pulled into its embroidered clutches.
Enchanted petals open to the morning sun
illuminating pollen.
Fledglings mouths
eager and wide.
A sprinkle of joy.
Not lost in the first bite.

Hospitality

Some will pour you into a chipped cup.
Their imprint imbued on a dull motif.
A vexed motive.

Others prepare a silver tray
decanting you into cut glass
that sparkles.
Chiming as it meets brilliant light.
Releasing the refinement of your bouquet.

I Remember the Specks of Bran

I remember the specks of bran in the dough
like her freckles becoming part of the mix.
She kneaded it as we needed her
to produce something to warm the heart.
The thick Ballyvaughan flag in front of the fire
never warmed.
That was the 80's harsh.
We were a trio
like a three ring circus with my sister.
We came together on a Friday night.
It felt like it was after the show
but Gaybo was on the television.
I often knelt on the green chair at the kitchen table.
As the envious night sky pressed against the teak window.
Making lush coleslaw from cabbage leaves.
And dainty queen cakes to sit on the long table
watched by tapestries that hang in my mind still.

My enthusiasm on tip toes trying to touch their gold leaf verges.
Muddling back over the locked school gates.
A match girl
where I hid beneath the bow of a smile
until the bell was taken out of the box.

I float back in time
on a worn velvet cushion
when my life is in ashes.

And feel the glow beneath a sense of worth
as solid as the flag dug out from the side of a battered hill.

And eat soda bread
with a trickle of butter over my lip.
All great things are lost in their indulgence
but some memories cut through the reality
and settle in the speckled fortress of my heart.

Futility

Entangled and frightened.
More part of the web
than part of the world
subdued.

The Splendour of Uncertainty

The splendour of uncertainty.
Having nodded my way through a row of caveats.
Slipping away like wings on a dandelion.
Thinking I know something about time and face.
A butterfly on the wing.
No mutiny.
Just a ravine I jumped while others slept.
Knowing sky is sky
and although your feet are clay
a beam of light can go anywhere.
Even bending its way into an old soul
illuminating a child's drawing.

Hardy Beach

Hardy beach
rolling out your watery carpet
on the moon's time sheet
not mine.
And I waiting for the second half
when you move down the field of sand.
To see foamy tide
leaving a puzzle of water snails.
Dressing the tilted wet floor
in a beggar's rag of seaweed
for a poor man's garden.
Flower snatched from a watery grave
by your bejewelled tide.
Offering shells and carving caves
where birds will nest
and no man can land
except the brave.
Salt water settles for a few hours
and then as if behind the plough you go again and sweat it out.

Hands are held over you
as if they could make a blossom grow.
Wanting to leave footprints in each others lives
that could be discovered on a family tree by their ancestors.

Black bog oak like ancient turtles seems to crawl.
This was a field once
but you have nestled into its darkness.

Perhaps it knew a real plough
before you hemmed it in
laying bare its roots.
A salting midas in all you touch.
And I trying to paddle back up stream
like an old salmon.
My thoughts like seagulls
searching the spray
for something I thought I saw.
Understanding little.
Only that I will come again
and warm my heart
in the bitter cold waters that rush against me.
And I thinking of the tug of war I raged
beyond the hardy beach and
holding on to a fist of sand
as extra time is called on a late Spring evening.

The Celtic Tiger

The European circus (IMF) came to town.
Three ring circuses tame tigers
and play with obtuse mirrors.
I sat on the verge of the seat
at the bank manager's office.
He offered me a ladder.
Not chrome plated or extendable
but for social climbing.
I peered out my apartment window.
I could imagine it drifting into the clouds
if I had the beans.
My utilities swinging this way and that in space.
I never saw the bubble.
When it burst my innards were exposed.
The bank manager had a retirement watch that didn't rewind.
I stood outside the circus field
as the lights flashed.
"Mummy are tigers real?"
"Tigers only eat lion tamers darling.
Watch the girl on the high wire
and pray she doesn't have to test the net."

Writing

I will scribble with my pen and paper
like hard water with poor soap.
It will lather eventually
and thoughts will slip from my mind.
Bubbling up and staining the page
with silky smooth and jagged edged
impressions of my reality.
Like a man with a shovel
digging into earth
and bringing up the undergrowth
and throwing it in imperfect lumps
over his shoulder
and it settling
like a drill of potatoes
bountiful with humility.

We All Hide

We all hide
in the wide open.
Those crowded spaces
where we can be in the crowd.
Physically.
The thinking ache is subdued
by our ability to glide with others.
To show boat
seamlessly.
Apparently on the same page.
Our collectivity brings a certain unanimity.
Confirmation that others chose
as we did.
And we are okay at that moment.

Stubborn Onions

Stubborn onions grew by the stone wall
before I built the extension.
Year after year their tough bulbs persisted.
A deep seeping aroma.
Peeling one
after another after another
at the kitchen sink.
They were stinging me on the inside
sort of.
I was allergic I think.
Until I decided I wanted to look out at flowers.
Food for bees.
Food for my senses.
Something sweet.
And so I did.
I dug the last onion.
But onions are never gone.

Even now buried beneath the extension.
There is tension.
Sitting here on concrete
two feet deep
I have my layers too.
Just in case
the flowers didn't grow
but they thrived.

Rocky Home of My Words

Rocky home of my words.
Sand like powdered gold.
Froth like whipped cream
soaking into a rink of clay.
I tip closer
to run like a coffin bay pony.
The rebellious breeze tugs at my security.
Icy waters from strange lands
mingle with old rivers.
I am an oxen on a rope
pulling against the moon.
My senses battling elements.
I feel the hold of mud.
The world is muted
like a bell that has lost its tongue to rust.
No lighthouse to serenade a skipper with its morse.
Yet God is with me always
close to the brink.
Where lifers stood and not for fun.

Life's spark ignites a desire to float endlessly
and dive deep into a breathless place.
To leave my bitterness in a salted tea.
To cure in the hands of time.
Almost consumed.
I pour myself back into life's britches
and hurry home.

Looking Back

Security
Erases fear in its infancy
before it climbs into the memory.

Younger Sisters Believe

Younger sisters believe.
We thought them to
pass it on.
Even when we were muddled
by the mundaneness.
We searched for lost pencils, non existent ribbons, their sparkle.
When they came the washing was already on the line.
She was in her stride.
We dreamed we were beautiful winged godmothers.
Harnessing the love.
Nurturing with time
we had to borrow.
Like old delph to them
patterns fading as sentimentality grew.
And then we flew.
I went to Trinity.
The cobbles felt like home.
Country you know.
And I perched
under a wing
in heels and a long pvc jacket.

Sunday nights
we felt their closeness
Ignite
on the back step
as they waved.
We re-entered the fire.

When we could have played ball
and everything still seems to burn.
Gentle like a purr
from the neighbour's marmalade cat.
And then unexpectedly
I choke on the fumes
like an old Aga.

When I see them now for coffee on the green.
Well dressed.
Pounding with life.
I seem to gleam
in the knowing
that it was they
who made I me
that and dear old pvc.

Rush from Page to Page

Rush from page to page
or read it twice.
Let it sink down into the mud
like only boots can.
Take the meaning like the imprint
not of your boot but of your soul.
Longing to take another step
but forwards means downwards.
Surrounded by
more memories than dreams now.
The scales tipping,
slipping from your hands.
Small short crocuses close to the webbed earth
grow beneath the yellowing sun.
Frolic in the bitter cold breeze.
More than still life.
You in your twilight.
Wounded.
Cut like a diamond.
Live.
Till every drop of living light has shone.

The Lost

There is a sort of braille
in the unknown
when you are barefoot so to speak.
The lost can read it.
It's dotted on the journey.
Some are trapped there on the road.
Looking for their failings on the retreat.
As if they could unlock a passageway.
Strugglers.
Swapping with others who
are aware of borrowed time
and how quickly sand shifts.
They engage when they sense the frequency of humility.
A gentle speak, children hear.
Journeyers walking into a thicket
with the certainty of air.
And
that means life ripples on.

The Second

There is an expectation that
'the second'
does not cut the sulphur.
A lesser equal.
Coming after the credits.
It flits with humility
and earns its ground.
It does not take the shape of the first
and must make way for boats to pass.
But oh, when it unfurls its sail
how it floats.
Like a maiden voyager bound for adventure.
On a deluge that lays float to captains when they
spy their second mate.

Yarns That Are Spun

Yarns that are spun
are unspun when company leaves.
Old friends feel their way through language.
That is more gist and melancholy and monologue
than the toing and froing
of acquaintances politely quarrelling.
Gathering words like ears of corn
to settle
behind the galvanise in the barn.
Finding themselves in friendship's deep waters.
Their minds
in an invisible tether.
Murmurings
resurfacing on a perishing tide.
Rocking chairs in silent company
knowing secrets that cannot be stolen.
Unfinished words opening a heart
as they leave the throat
hoarse.
Each syllable letting loose its meaning
as easy as a breeze
causes leaves to detach and circulate
without any mechanism other than
the pull of the natural.

Hedgehog

A pin cushion.
Little more.
Tapping.
Through unswept leaves.
On twi-lit glass.
Filling the vestibules of my heart
with longing.
My tilted head promising.
As if I knew the lock or a conifer filled den of innate rumblings.
Hunger fear.
Like my young, climbing onto my tattered lap.
Ever chattering.
And then in an instant settling.
Like a sand sculpture barely real
And they not seeing
the vastness, the tenderness
the tapping
of the lost in me.

Marooned

On a corner I stood.
A captain looking out through a magnifying glass into the swell.
In charge of the gang plank.
News was funnelled to me
by those who passed.
I decided their fate.
Second chance cigarettes were smoked.
They were as lame as my engine.
I was destined to drift.
I could gauge how well I was doing by the strength of my back
against the breeze
but I was drowning on the inside.
Waves of emotion hitting me over and over.
I had my compass.
It shone in the dark.
A hungry sea dog at my feet tired.
I couldn't leave this block.
A roofless dreamer my mind wouldn't be still.
Constantly throwing something up on the surf.
I maintain the captaincy on the corner of two streets.
Only room for one at the top.
Thirsty in an ocean
but I couldn't access a drop
of freshly brewed tea.

Sea gulls would circle.
I never left my pew.
Men in white coats, white noise screeching across the sky.
White light.
Telling me what they could see.
An old man on the corner of nobody street.
Not blending in with the facade.
I would ask for this one and that.
A humble ships mate to put down my anchor
and record stories of journeys
yet to be travelled.
A reassuring smile
bobbing on the candour of a nodding chin.
Telling me I wasn't shipwrecked on no man's land
but that the nets were full
and I stayed the course.

Cocooned

Morning tea rocked on an uneven stone
a little cold.
Holding paperwork in place.
Flapping like a trapped bird.
A bulging cocoon struggling with its inhabitant.
Imagination spluttering into life.
A slow release
from a warping blade of grass.
Spilling dew down onto thirsty earth.
Between two rocks a line of slime
signifies a journey.
Glimmering in dancing sunlight.
Nobody around but me.
A bird on a berry bush bleating and then silenced in a twitch
of his wing.
My eyes hovering like a dragonfly
waiting at an interchange.
Bees shooting past like fat powerful land rovers.
Thriving on instinct and the scent of success.
Like those beyond the fence.
Conquering the tarmac.
Outbound.
Not following a snails trail.
And I marooned on a therapeutic island in my mind.
Dragging my heels against the seeds
I had forgotten I planted in the Spring.
Nothing visible but a bare soul.

Balancing myself and leaning against the moss dressed wall
as if all the garden were a cradle.
Waiting for a sapling to spy a chink of light
and break the surface tension with a sprinkle of crushed
marietta and a gentle breeze.
Spurning her little chick
lifting the latch and teaching her
to spread her green tinged palms
and take flight in her size fives.

Visiting Aran

When I visited the Aran Islands
I felt Irish.
There was a baptism so to speak
on the boat.
The captain said we were going against the tide.
I felt unsettled.
I couldn't see the mainland, only the clouds drifting to the
America's.
My identity was shifting.
Red and blue rusted tug boats were tied up with ancient knots
like unsolved riddles.
I could smell the catch.
Boats named like shanty towns.
I remember 'An Sagart'.
I didn't know if I was part of the tribe.
My brogue
meeting soft linguistic twists of locals
depending on tourists.
And we sat on a heap of stones against a barn
wondering about hiring bikes.
Out to sea there was nothing but rolling surf.
I could feel the pages of history turning.
I wanted to go slow.
And so we walked.
I had my German cousins with me.
They were accustomed to travel.

I had a desire to find myself
in an abandoned window into history somewhere.
I knew it would be in the West.
I could feel symmetry I couldn't see.
Hoisted by my ancestors.
I was reassured by an old man
that the path goes in circles.
And if I got lost there would only be one light in the evening.
The lighthouse
And I should go the opposite way.
I'm not sure if he was tired of invaders
with backpacks stealing their stones.
The generational tether was weakening and needed to be
buttressed much more than stone cottages.
There was little time.
I returned years later and stayed up all night.
Reading epic poems, and stories of local legends.
Their legacy always on the rebirth.
I could not find him
Only an automated lemon light devoured by waves.
I knew by then I could leave a rock at any shore
As all roads go round.
And that I would not write or dream until I touched down in
West Clare.

Roisin Veronica Horgan read law at Trinity College Dublin and divides her time between her dual passions of Mediation and Writing. She lives close to the Shannon Estuary in County Clare, Ireland.

In this, her first collection, she explores what home means to her and captures its essence with a sensitive lens. Her poetry is brimming with evocative visual delights, personal insights and a deep sense of respect for place, memory, displacement and the journey home.

Lightning Source UK Ltd.
Milton Keynes UK
UKHW020831060223
416538UK00016B/1785

9 781782 229124